IN ARENA AND AROMA OF WORDS

REFLECTIONS SPOKEN TO PRINT

By

MARTIN HACKLEMAN

CITI OF
BOOKS

CITIOFBOOKS, INC.
3736 Eubank NE Suite A1
Albuquerque, NM 87111-3579
www.citiofbooks.com

Hotline:	1 (877) 389-2759
Fax:	1 (505) 930-7244

Ordering Information:
Quantity sales. Special discounts are available on quantity purchases by corporations, associations, and others. For details, contact the publisher at the address above.

Printed in the United States of America.

ISBN-13:	Paperback	979-8-89391-625-6
	eBook	979-8-89391-627-0
	Hardback	979-8-89391-626-3

Library of Congress Control Number: 2025906685

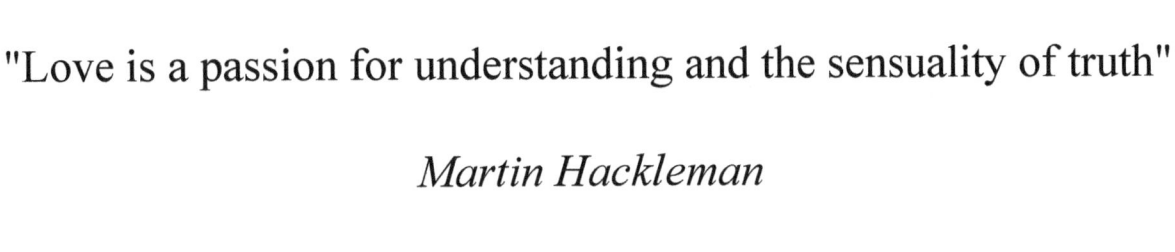

"Love is a passion for understanding and the sensuality of truth"

Martin Hackleman

AUTHOR BIO

Martin Hackleman, a world-renowned French horn player, began his distinguished career at the remarkable age of 19 as Principal Horn of the Calgary Philharmonic. He went on to hold the same prestigious position with the Vancouver Symphony, Montreal Symphony, and the National Symphony Orchestra at the Kennedy Center in Washington, D.C., solidifying his status as one of the finest horn players of his generation.

Internationally acclaimed, Hackleman toured the world as a member of both the Canadian Brass and the Empire Brass Quintet. His extensive discography includes over 50 professional albums, featuring orchestral works, chamber music, and numerous solo recordings.

Now retired from his role as Professor of Horn at the University of Missouri-Kansas City's Conservatory of Music, Hackleman lives in Kansas City with his wife, Kelly, and their two Mini Golden Doodles, Kenna and Duncan.

TABLE OF CONTENTS

PRELUDE

I love words. While they are technically just air vibrations bouncing off our eardrums, they ignite involuntary responses of questions, empathy, irritation, and care to infinite levels in us all. Words are tangible. They can conjure heat, cold, light, and darkness. Colors often abound, and even smells can waft up with some toppings of fear.

Our lives are a series of walks into various experience rooms, sometimes on purpose and sometimes by accident. This leaves us with different sensations and questions that we later try to explain to ourselves with an aged, banged-up memory in words either written by us or someone else for us to read. Looking over our shoulders is the definition of experience.

Much of what I talk about is familiar to us all. But here, I am a personal gardener, tending these roses and weeds, using different spades and shovels just as others might too. The foliage is recognizable and universal. These words are my take on common questions and answers on both ends of my life.

The book is basically two sections that are an early time in my life and the older contemporary time I live in now - my life as bookends. The first part, "Poems from a Young Heart," is a specific snapshot period in my youth, from age 17 to 24. To better understand all the classic turmoil that we all feel at that age, I, for some strange reason, just started writing poetry.

The Arena, in the title, is the emotion room, the circumstance, and ramification of some parts of living, thought upon. Some of my locutions have obvious sharp points of the question, and others just have subtle breaks and bumps in a sidewalk of understanding. I hope you keep reading, enjoying, and watching your step.

The Aroma infers, often circumspect, what words can evoke in us, both individually and in tribes of paragraphs. That involuntary emotional evocation is like remembering bacon in the morning - unavoidable.

I never had any premeditation or ambition to write other than to have it serve as a personal cathartic mechanism for me to gain some deeper understanding and peace within my own head. There is nothing unique about all this except that it was, to me, in my early writing, experiencing the first confusing tidal wave of time in my own personal young space. My questions and fears daily sucked the air out of whatever room I was in.

After the simplicity of the open-mouthed, smooth-skin youth, this older youth was inexplicably seeing only questions, passions, and beauty. Pimples of experience appeared in the mirror. My mouth was now mostly pursed lips and eyes staring blankly instead of experiencing those effortless young smiles and wide eyes I used to know. Now, my eyes were suddenly fixed on out-of-focus variables and questions instead of the joyful toys I used to so easily grasp. Before, it was sandboxes, but suddenly, it began to feel like sandstorms.

I was operating on a diet of perplexing and heated young questions. I felt by writing I was talking to myself, and this allowed me liberty to "say things" in a language that I could not actually state out loud. Those personal Deus ex Machina sets of words, which I constructed out of desperation and wonderment back then, often bumped into my daily life before it made things better. I began to learn instead of just experience.

The second part of the book is me about 50 years later, reflecting in a slightly less poetic but still evocative style on what I have learned…contemplating what I achieved on purpose and by mistake. Much of that nubile young passion ended up sustaining me as I trudged and soared. Now, I can naturally sense a conclusion, and writing again helps me understand and accept what I am feeling. I did not write much for several years because I was very busy in my musical career and really could not take my eyes off my career path. Looking back at the young words next to the older words is interesting.

I am sharing what I hoped and aimed for back then, along with the well-basted and slow-cooked reality that I now have. Some may find my writing too clever, ambiguous, or odd; "Just say it!" comes to mind. If, after reading this Prelude, you find that odor too pungent, you are fortunate not to waste any more time, as this short introduction will be enough to send you packing.

I am simply asking questions that can have answers with causes that show no favor or blame. I am trying to see and accept. I am talking out loud to myself. If you do it when no one is around, you are not crazy.

I hope you enjoy my bookend thoughts from youth to experience.

Part One:

Poems from a Young Heart

6/16/70

Thee

I saw a dog laid prostrate by death
along the road this morn, this fine morn,
the sun baking the motionless eternity into the pavement.
Only the sun's flies upon the inflamed instantaneous horror
there cast upon the metallic path.
Streaming like steel tears around the corpse,
the breathing fast iron running close to a marathon,
in speedy memoriam, the pistons humming an elegy
by the thousands.

7/25/70

Youth is gone when innocence is recognized as an act
and years are more than time.
When trying must be qualified thrice and hairs split instead of combed.
When distaste is more the rule than the exception and you grow bitter
with time.
When religion turns to a body, no longer attitudes but dogmatic
sacraments,
an all possessive delirium of yesterdays, trepidation, and tomorrows.
When complacency enters more than the vocabulary she is gone.

9/20/70

Mirror, I see me in your silver sea.
Quickly you follow each blink and catch every glance
no matter how hard I try to keep one to myself.
In an instant, as long as I wish,
Looking away, I am evaporated from your easel and now must look back
to the corner of my eyes and the drapery of shut lids to see my heart
for in you words mean nothing, could be a yawn, could be a sneeze.
As fleet as my body and time, I fill your space to see
tears and their tracks, shadows in movements
and sometimes, sometimes a queer angle to the sky,
hoping to see what I should have missed.
Silver sea, are you only a pane, part of the game, or are you the fate of us
all?
Only reflection our end and instant our call?
I pray, let my fraction and memory gust to whomever
be a framed desire, not really only mortal accomplishment.
Remember me as I prayed and not in the flesh colors of a box.
Reflect, if you will, upon my goal, for often my days were ill to my
crusade.
I after all, only human, like you, only a love.
That is no victory but a path so clear that it could only lead to peace.

12/21/70

Slowly the clocks hands take people from the womb by the throat
and decapitate a fragile body from an eternal soul.
Rotting minds numbed by too many sunsets and mauled by too many
mornings.
Wrinkled days of memory canes and pills of prayer and sleep.
My brittle days shall come and I shall be a relic of love but please put
me low
upon the shelf so I can see the sun through the window.

12/27/70

Father

There was a boy, a man who breathed adolescent peace.
Mature love his style, through days of dark and mistakes of nails
all he did not deserve.
His heart be more royal than the skies color he loves so much and
wider than horizon suns.
Though reprise to his hands be taut, they still hold gently
a child's face and save good days as real meaning.
Consistent flexible strength today hewn tomorrow
a more gentle monument and forge glyphic masterpieces of the past,
so our souls would not fast.
Whose intensity does not often burn narrow to impatience
but a collected beam.
Roots of insight with eyes that cherish each face and tree.
From the mornings wisdom to the evenings prayer a wise man, a
student.
A giant that weeps, a rose, a peak, with petals saline,
a little less perfection but much more a man,
he is my father, the days of my life.

2/12/71

I tend to think that I will not find by seeking,
digging at my heart with catalyst dreams, molds, and expectations.
She shall come as a sudden rain and as through as the wind.
Her smile will be my day and she will erase me from me.
Her name shall be my soul.

3/27/71

If I said I love you would you laugh
and send me away, my heart wrapped in thirsty words, wind the only
reply?
If I said I love you would you bid I stay and leave no lash unturned,
no breath churning without the other near to guide the reply through lips
and other gifts?
Would you bid I stay and love to a death which I neither see nor you?
The endings fault be that we did not die the first day we loved and there
loved forever.

7/10/70

Maturity is simply choosing which characteristics
of childhood should be removed, which should remain,
and somehow retaining a spontaneity that left days ago
unnoticed and scared.

6/10/71

The Writer

There are men with minds and there are minds
who have men.
A writer seems to be a prisoner of the alphabet,
a free man in frustration whose days are but toiling paragraphs.
The metallic snap of a typewriter arm slapping the fleshy
rubber roll with tongueless words, dreams humbled to print.

8/20/72

Politics

What maker of society would have guessed that the forum he
strove to create would be the perverted pedestal that is now our
hierarchy of sycophants, nadir of most honesty?
Forensic ambitions create blueprints of rationalized facts
that twists simplicity into grotesque blindness.
Leaders being led by a piqued mass that is by nature
unreadable, unspeakable, and unleadable.

12/6/73

For a young man I feel very old.
For what have I spoken that did not coast by my words
down ambivalent predestined paths.
For what I have written that was best left
to bleached paper and imaginations pen.
Where have I gone that did not lead me
to where I was, miles that didn't count.
A very secure sameness and help that was a technicality of
interference.
Whom can I say I've touched but age, seen but effort?
It's that strain that leaves me better but weaker.
Like an animal stretching his arm between the bars
we ask for tomorrow because we hope, no we know, there must be
more.

6/25/75

When I was a young man I used to sit around writing my loneliness
into crowds of words that talked to one another as poems.
A negative word would juxtapose a little syllable of hope,
tomorrow butt up against an old hot night.
Those words lifted my sadness, my personal empty road, up to
believing
That the mornings map was a working trip that would see me to a
new city.
I have worked and grown better, waited and grown bitter.
This is the experience that forges patience and spends days.
Youth spent for age, age dying for youth.
The wisdom of acceptance is quiet

10/9/69

Wind

You were here first. You never aged or needed to change.
You never faltered, loved or hated.
You always touch, always enhance.
Neither light nor dark hinders your aim and
you expertly reconfigure the clouds eternally.
You are the breath of birds, the playmate of rain
and you never get in the way of the stars.
You and your cousin water cannot be stopped
and generally, help in beautiful ways,
as your first duty.
You express a caress like the gentle back of a hand
or a puff to rearrange hair.
I love walking with you while you
talk to my breath, your dear cousin.

11/19/69

I dream to bathe in its molten wax,
be purged and baptized in its flawless flame.
To climb its wick and frolic in its warm sea.
Then someone blows out the candle
and I am suspended in the wax as is the flame.

1/27/70

When skin diminishes and time takes a firm grip
by sturdy decades hair changes color to the autumn man.
Movements slow to catch the details youth so fleetingly missed.
The old are left with very little if you call all the words
of a compounded grown spring,
every wisp and storm, memory, gust and breeze a trifle.
But look into the eyes and you will see
all age has left is the sincerity of youth's words.

1/26/70

When you tire of the combat with the snarling radio
and are too badly bruised from the traffic crawling on your mind,
picking and shredding at days hope, leaving it like
bleached wheat, silence helps.
When a tear is forgotten or even remembered,
a thought mistook or misplaced, laid scattered
amongst various other words, silence helps.
Noise is like a dirty bandage.
Silence helps if first the wound is cleaned with clear sincerity.

4/27/70

Wouldn't it be grand if all the world were ruled by words?
If words were decree the movement would be so fast.
Up and down in a matter of breath, instant in and out
and death would be so painless.
"I love you" and it would be done,
 "die" and it would come,
infinity reduced to context.
But words don't, we do, and that's the real reason for tears.

5/4/70

Soliloquy;
A man has his smile.
How personal, faint, and pristine
must a soul be to let such a harbinger sing.
The erosion of joy slants that smile astray
and the soliloquy of hope is exeunt with the wind.
A phantom, he comes in an instant

7/13/70

Death, you are the prayer of a silent prisoner,
singing winged echoes down forgotten halls,
through Gothic rooms hung heavily with tapestries of chain.
You are the shadow in fog, she who wavers in the lull of a wind storm.
Arriving in a vortex no one feels, then lingers on top the cold.
Silence is her script and she writes upon imagination
epic pains that bleed loneliness and yesterday.
She is the conquered conquerer, the fair and foul,
the depth of a laceration.
She is the far close of an instant and the tonality of eternity.
She is my fascination and all our end
The meaning of never
that art has twisted to forever.
She waits in black corners, inhabiting forgotten books breathing
a seething theme between a cover no one wants to open,
no one wants to read but everyone sees on a shelf.

6/30/71

Driving down a road aimlessly in the night,
at a stop-light, a girl in the car to my left
born just seconds before my intersection hesitation,
mouthing the words of the song on the radio
I was hearing too.
Behind her closed glass she blankly stared into my open windows
of pouring solitude.
She knows the ideas and speech by repetition and takes the frequency
passions as an intimate lover.
Or possibly only regurgitates the noise through involuntary lips,
the squeak of a dry mind rolling down a road.
Through ears the passions poured and into the mind they settled.
Now her mouth chews that muse
and out they drool for the ears to digest.
Circular meals in the night at a stop-light.

7/3/71

I put my ear-phones on and disconnected them from noise.

As they sat over my ears I could hear less of the air-conditioner drone,

night rodents, and the other people.

I could hear my teeth play with my tongue

and hear my blood rush when I clenched my jaw.

I hear my heart when I hold my breath.

I hear so much because I hear so little.

My eyes see easier and as I

write it seems as though my mind is imagining wilder.

I can hear the symphonies of deaf men, see the sprint of the cripple,

and observe bright sunsets of the blind.

Many people are ruled by their senses and the chaos they can breed,

their soul emptying through environment and repetition.

This peace is so valuable because it is so often unattainable.

What a beautiful journey that is as close as silence.

8/8/71

Sleep, you sentinel of my sanity,
fashion now my frame in still.
As silence becomes a cat, unsheathe rapier dreams to soot
disappointments with verisimilitudes and run through tomorrow's fears
to the bone along with today's failures.
Pattern capricious movements in your patient style
and behind your valance let darkness teach me renewal,
for the suns crushing blows come in waves of toil.
My insular flesh has limits as measure, struggling effigy that fears,
but breath is the speech of the soul.
Let my soul talk with the Shiva while my carcass
abides in capitulation and blessed mortal sleep.

8/21/71

What will become of my words?
Will they stray to an untrue path and nestle into obscurity?
Will fate ever open my page with a finger of wisdom?
Will these linguistic swirls fade,
passions pen not tipped in acumen and sagacity?
Will they pale under times sure heat
and be reduced to a fast white as they began?
Will I only nod to these puzzles peace,
as my personal parts never fit for you?

9/6/71

There is no greater tribute one can pay to stark experience
than by attaining a flexible set of colorful opinions.
There is no greater life than dedicated stains of sincere effort.
The preceding is the only non-flexible opinion
I strive to incorporate in my swirling days of banal beauty.

10/3/71

When I am happy I know how much more effective
I could be if your hand had formed my smile.
With you time is a friend of intimacy.
No matter how I feel there is always more to it,
always with direction in your company.
To know of you is to know for you
and by this living perfectly even in your absence,
but in your presence,
but in your presence.

9/12/71

When you are not in the car the radio talks,
no malmsey to my senses and traveling in thirst..
I don't smile often without your shadow
upon my efforts and only laugh
when I am able to smile with your personality near.
More and more I feel I might implode without you.
You look me in the eyes to see, not to be seen,
talk to listen and listen to see.
There are places to go in your presence,
and reasons to weep in your absence.
More and more I feel I might implode without you.

10/21/71

Throughout all my existence there has never been
any other person who gave so much of his own life
in order to give mine strength and direction.
You were security even in absence and
now strength that is my personality.
You were patience in my wrongs,
now, pray the wisdom of my love.
You were tenderness even in the tiniest touch,
now kindness I try to live.
You are my father, he who gives my soul the noble tradition.
As a matrix, soil to a seed, you are where I began
and though I may grow tall you forever hold my roots.

1/26/74

I would like to be a mirror to see man's true disgust
and observe his honest distrust.
To pierce that lusty eye
to a marrow of insecurity and honesty.
A fool cannot trick a fool in the quiet company of
one another's solitary audience.
That audience allows no masks.
The bitter brow crumbles under the translucent gaze
and has no response curtain to dart behind.
He stands naked in the man-made ice.
But in that dark portrait he senses
some bright or else he would not stand at all.
A state of siege on today's honest simplicity
is pitted against looking for what is not there.
For all the vain efforts, what poor cosmetics.

1/27/70

When skin diminishes time takes a firm grip with sturdy decades.
As hair changes color to the autumn man and movements slow
to catch the details youth so scrupulously missed.
The old are left with very little if you call all the words
of compounded springs memory gusts a trifle.
Look into the eyes and you will see
all age has left is the sincerity of youth's words.

Part Two:

Writings from an Aged Heart

FOUR HANDS AND TWO HEARTS

Now, after all these years, I have to have a real, frank conversation with myself regarding my relationship with my parents. I am not sure what I was really seeing in them with my half blind eyes of youth. I do know that I learned in spite of myself.

To me, remembering there were little episodes, interludes, where I sensed the love and care from each in different ways. I caught all their tender care in pungent whiffs. They reached out and embraced me, in all my young, personal confusion, combustion, and distraction, so beautifully and maturely within the bounds of their own personal turmoil. I am sure I missed the subtlety of their embrace often. I was distracted by my own whirlwind confusion caused by the inevitable mutation of body and emotion to see much else. This is not unique, and I am far from alone in this pattern.

Now, what I feel, at this skewed distant time, is maybe that they were also somewhat busy and distracted by each other's conceived and real short fallings, mutual angst, and requisite bickering. They were feeling disappointment for not loving one another as they had done so beautifully in the not-too- distant past. With age grows strengths but, at the same time, opportunities for the thin parts in ourselves to stretch and break. Expand the tangle of best intentions and weakness makes us all grow, inevitably, in uneven sowed fields.

I imagine now the hectic dreaming of their parenting. They lovingly look down upon the four lives they caused. And now, having to constantly watch for the potholes all four whirlwind children are creating at an alarming rate. So many plates to spin with only four hands and two hearts.

I sometimes felt alone and that they were too busy with their own demons. The timing of the explosion of all six of our unique but regular lives did not build a sufficient foundation of communication.

I take responsibility for being a quiet rouge. I did it out of not knowing who I was but knowing that I must bolt to something more. I am partially responsible for cutting them off, to a degree, through growth and natural desperation. The divorce that was exploding just as I was leaving to start my career was very decisive as well.

I am here now, resplendent in trial and triumph, and have a great fondness for my entire family. Thank you, Jay Kent and Doris.

REAL LIFE

4:05 PM. I am standing in the kitchen. Duncan dashes out to the back gate facing the garage and does his barking at the neighbor's cat, which only he sees. I pause to look out on a whim to see if I can finally see the feline felon. I see someone on a bike halfway into my garage.

My neighbor, an avid biker and always in the requisite Pachinko parlor bright colors that bikers wear to survive texting drivers, seems to be in my garage. I am like, "Why is Ken in my garage?" I walk out to the gate to understand the strange visit to find a wild man on a bike with my leaf blower in one hand, battery in the other, and a half empty bottle of whiskey in the third hand. I, of course, opened with the cordial greeting stating, "What the fuck are you doing!?" He glibly stated that he was broke and needed this leaf blower to do some intense leaf cleanup now that all the leaves had fallen and it was Winter. That is actually not what he explained to me. It was more along the lines of, "I 'm broke, and I need this, and if you don't give it to me, I will shoot you!" I told him I had some umbrage with the situation.

Actually, those were not the urtext words I conjured at the time. They were more accurately, "The fuck you are, get the fuck out of here, that is not yours!" We continued our repartee along similar lines until I said, "If you need the money, I will give you some." He dropped the four-foot leaf blower and battery from hands two and three, and then I paused and said, "What makes me think that you won't shoot me even if I give you some money?" He said, "I don't have a gun."

I reached into my wallet and gave him twenty dollars and told him to fuck off and that I was calling the cops. We exchanged convivial "fuck you's" as he sped off as quickly as one-armed drunk guy holding a whiskey could do. To tell the truth, he did better than I could have done drunk, one arm controlling a bike downhill, yelling over my shoulder. It was scary, but my adrenaline was turned on. I understand that mental illness and homelessness are tragic, but I can not let this desperate action stand.

I actually offered the money because I knew he did need it and that a twenty-dollar bill would probably be more than he could get for a leaf blower in December. I was pissed but sympathetic, if that can be a thing. He drove off down the street yelling profanities, but what I chose to hear was that he was yelling, "Thanks!" People who feel they have no choice but to dive into two feet of mental water need to be acknowledged and admitted to real life with our help. He did not want to be in my garage drunk on a bike.

However, I am sure that after the whiskey was gone, he could have done a fine job cleaning the recalcitrant nonexistent leaves from my yard.

IT WILL MAKE ITSELF CLEAR

I have found myself, so many times, at the front desk of life saying, "Please, Sir, what is Next?"

We all run hard, with focused conviction toward our goals, in our emotional wish cars. They often have low tires and half a tank of conviction, but hey, we are at least behind the wheel of something.

After hitting too many wicked, unexpected curbs and reacting a bit late to too many curves, we find we need to find a better road. Maybe it's because we are following a self-made map of hope and confusion drawn with disappearing ink.

I have found that it is paramount to move forward with conviction, character, and care, but to also often stop and stand on a corner of my scaffolding and say to myself, "Have some faith. It will make itself clear." There are actually so many deserved and underserved consequences and curves that cannot be seen that are best experienced on our Duct taped elevated platform of wishes, standing still and just looking out and up.

Take a breath and notice that you don't actually see all you really want or need. Don't rush to victory or sadness with presumptions and obese plans.

All our days open with leaving sleep and diving into necessity. Over coffee, The Plan remerges like indigestion, so take a Tums of patience and a slow, deep breath and proceed to the ruts you have laid out for yourself.

Try to see new, fresh places to plant your passion on today's horizon. How can I grow and help the ones around me at the same time? After a bit of age, we figure out that if we lend a hand, many palms will extend to us as well.

Be wise by letting today just lay there and greet you with that goofy grin. Proceed to make this haute de cuisine dumpster fire of dreams and realities called today a bit better than yesterday but not as good as tomorrow. Good will come as a beautiful breeze at the same time you stub your toe again.

THE EYES OF LIMPID APPRECIATION

I often see homeless persons on the edge of the streets, passed out on some corner, or collapsed in a vacant doorway. I used to think, "why don't you try?" Eventually, I realized that maybe what I was seeing was not not-trying but falling short with the short arrows they had in their quiver. My point here is that the ability for us to spark joy at any given moment is omnipresent and immensely significant. We should not just acknowledge the passing sadness that stands shoulder to shoulder with our own lucky, blessed personal joys and growth. We need to consider influencing the imbalance sometimes.

I was walking out of a grocery today and noticed a houseless person laying by the wall in a pool of stagnant, still despair, looking down at his hands, wondering, "why have you not pulled me from this?" I realized there was not much I could do to reverse this, not much I could do to fix this, not much that I could even do to understand this personal hell. However, there was one small thing I could do to bring a brief moment to help lift him from the cold cement to a small, emotional, warm embrace with a small monetary gift. This gift was not asked for but implied by sitting and leaning against a grocery store entry on a patch of cold cement, staring blankly.

Many troubled folks among us often extend hands, and we react often by looking forward and walking a bit more rigidly. We may even feel something in our warm cars that smacks of sympathy. The observed plight too often ends in a conundrum and a sad resignation that results in our passing stiffly by. But today, for one moment, I turned around to this brave, challenged soul, walked back, and gave him five dollars to do with whatever made his heart sing. I did not do this for any other reason than to let him, for a moment, see that there are moments when gentleness just is. Sympathy can breathe out, no matter how limited and infrequent. I am reporting this encounter for no other reason than to hope some others might quietly recognize this warm feeling and have some desire to replicate it. A hand extended for one in the near can go far for all.

FIND A FAN

I have a Hitachi electric fan that is at least 30 years old. It is in my home studio now, where I play my guitar and meditate, now at 71 and retired. This room is my overall favorite place to hang in our big, old 1908 house. Whenever I go into that room, that fan comes on. I rarely need the actual blustery airy machinations it unleashes, but rather seek its singing sound.

The gentle rush of its little motor voice is a refreshing malmsey to the teetering doubt that seems to hang in too many of my silent corners. Now, I need to explain I LOVE fans. From my early childhood experiences in a very hot Texas, where there were mostly only hard, sweltering days partnered with long, sweaty nights, we did not know that things could be any other way and consequently gave it no thought.

All four of us kids felt fortunate to have one sacred room in the house where we grew up that was blissfully air conditioned with a single stalwart window unit - this champion was in the dining room. Who likes eating meatloaf sweating? But our bedrooms were, unfortunately, a converted area in the attic with only an open window on either end, so fans were our saviors, our best friends. I realized that I craved the fan's constant whisper, Siren singer, with her gentle, constant purr and loving expression of air that breathed over my withering, tacky body.

My first fan love affair was with a large box fan my grandmother had in Bryan, Texas. I still have it. It's a Sears & Roebuck solid wood box fan that is three feet wide, three feet tall, and a foot deep, about twenty-five pounds, with single aluminum louvers you had to adjust individually. It was my best friend. I was at a considerable young age at this point. That, along with my status within the myriad of the siblings/cousin's hierarchy, left me consequently sleeping on the floor of a sitting room.

There was not much of a bed, but more like a mat. Because I weighed all of 20 pounds soaking wet, I did not know I was uncomfortable. But my grandmother, in her divine wisdom, for some reason, let me have control of this bodacious Sears fan. I quickly put it six inches from the top of my innocent, inexperienced little head at bedtime.

This fan's speed choices were impressive. The speeds on this puppy went from a gentle Bahamian afternoon siesta to full-on Tropic Tornado that parted my hair hard and blocked out all sound. I was literally blown away. I had peace and coolness in that hot Texas town that was life changing.

As time went on, in all the places where I have lived, I have had a fan nearby, even in winter. When I traveled and did not have my whispering breeze box, I often wore earplugs to create a breathing sound that mimicked my beloved fan's language.

All these decades later, I still exhale an inner sigh every time I turn on my fan. I hope we all can find that fulcrum of personal history/inner peace that we can connect to. Some of us do it involuntarily, out of some ancient youthful bliss, but most of us must consciously raise this Genie from a memory bottle in order to inhale its peace and waft in its nectar to transport us.

We all have our fans somewhere, so please find a fan that you can be a fan of!

KICKING THE CAN
DOWN THE ROAD

We all know what this means. Putting it off, "There will be a better time," "I 'm not ready," "I can't handle this right now," too many other things are more important.

When we are young, as kids, we do not know of this option. Someone says you go do this now, and you go do it. As we mature, we start to see the natural evolution of the copious lists of living. Too many classes, too many friends, new interests that sparkle with adrenaline, excitement, and lust. And we start noticing small shoots of ambition protruding out of some of these trinkets.

We naturally start to understand the art of prioritization. We develop careers and families that, at night, we reminisce, ponder, and smile at. Middle age cans have tight, svelte, mature plastic lids that hold in the imaginings and dreams pretty well, so no liquid care leaks with our punts.

As time proceeds, the cans vary in size, and some of their lids seem almost welded from the regular dusty relegation of getting to know our feet. Some are all the way off the path, to the side, in the little gutter of time and growth that life naturally digs for us.

After decades, we have collected quite a bevy of various containers strewn in our path. After a while, it sometimes feels better just to step over some of them rather than deliver another well-practiced toe kiss.

Then, one day, you see so many containers, all dented and rusty, on the old path, but you also sense, on the horizon, a looming end to your dirt rug runner of life. Now, some of the old tiny metal barrels we now gaze upon are dear objects that we really want to pick up and open.

Now we are at this late action of popping off the old lids and smelling the fecund contents, hoping there is no rot so we can finally feast on some of those dreams. Does it smell like sauerkraut or cherries?

The realization that many of our old ways don't work when we are old, gob smacks us like learning Santa wasn't real. We now need to give ourselves the gift of not waiting. Do it. Spend it. Live it. Savor it. Remember it for as long as you can. Don't wait.

LAST RECITAL

Not MY recital but witnessing a gentle presentation of one of my accomplished young master's students who I feel proud of. It's just the timing of HIS particular recital that coincides with me hitting the brick wall of my teaching full time coming to an end.

We all hit brick walls. Sometimes, it's out of the blue, and sometimes slowly approaches in full sight. Through living, there are barriers and walls that we encounter that we have to bound over, skip around, and sometimes just quickly and adroitly avoid.

With youth, we can see distant alternative paths and other approaches and landing strips. We have seemingly endless time to sort it out and come up with a plan. But as age piles on valuable experience, it adds weight as well. I don't mean the thicker visceral meat we lug around, but rather a short breathed hesitation we have learned with that extended time. We are slower to pick things up. Sometimes, that wisdom comes with too many scars.

Careers have their length, contract in time, and fervor. I feel so fortunate to have been able to hang on to my personal steering wheel of Fate for most of the time in my life. When one has a focused passion, even Fate's advice can be brushed aside out of personal dedication.

There certainly have been numerous significant moments when I had to wrest the helm from Fate's bony hands, but I am happy and a bit surprised to say it seems to have fought less than I would have thought. Maybe because it begrudgingly knew I knew better because of my sinew passion. It is as though there were times it smiled down on me and saw I could live with my own choice, even as I might be sailing over a cliff.

Life is a series of chapters, plateaus, and acts. We all learn the lines at the time and speak to whom we need to in order to get on with our plan and agenda. We do not know how many acts we will have. This gentle, genuine, beautiful little recital was an apogee for this budding talent that just happened to coincide with the end of my full-time teaching.

Now I am looking forward to creating my own priorities that have personal heft in my private life that are not as publicly poised as in my past career. Looking into myself for inspiration and gazing into my beautiful partner's eyes to appreciate the incredible love I have so serendipitously stumbled into to last my eternity.

PARENTING 101

At some time in my grade school youth, I ran across a unicycle in the garage. I don't know where or how it got there, but this bucking bronco, a simple single wheel vehicle from hell, was looking at me, laying on the ground, saying, "Want to take a ride, bitch?" Now, here's young me, gazing with a cocked head and pursed lips, hearing loudly a Siren Song of curiosity.

I am, at this age, ignorant, fearless, clueless, and seemingly invincible. Other than the fear of some specter under the bed, I had no idea I was unknowingly a SuperMan that was blessed upon me by not knowing any better. No one cared or really even knew I was about to take up a Balancing Wheel from Hell.

I propped myself up on a car in the driveway and shoved off, leaning forward and pedaling with the intensity that always left me on the pavement in spite of my sincerity. I gradually got better and learned that it came down to leaning slightly forward and pedaling just enough to almost catch up to your head.

I actually got good enough to occasionally deliver papers using two hands to throw papers on both sides of the street. But then, one day, I carelessly left my victory in the driveway behind my mother's car. She did not see it and ran over it. My dreams of riding a unicycle, juggling in a circus were, literally, crushed. Actually, I didn't really have that dream, but up to the car incident, it could have been an option.

Note here, in those days, most of the time; the mom was the lone sentry overseeing these riptide volcanoes of cuteness and hell. Also, in those days, taking care of the kids amounted to often opening the back door and saying, "Have fun!" It was really most often, "Give me a break." I am not saying that my parents did not love and cherish me, but they too were going on gut love and hope, with judgments they inherited, both good and bad.

And there were four kids and about 10 plates spinning at any given time. Germs were our middle name and if you could get up, you were fine. Back then, there were few helmets or pads, emotionally or physically.

I know my parents cared for us all, but we all were on long leashes, if tethered at all. I think there is a lot to be said for playing on your own and sometimes chasing some caprice interest unsupervised. I hope that young people today can find their own unicycle to teeter upon and eventually go for a spin.

SILENCE IS LOUD

The behemoth symphony is suddenly silenced by the conductor's swipe, and the concert hall is swallowed by a giant silence. This is the antithesis of what they thought they paid for and an emotional roar they never expected.

Two people have reached a point that has been loudly percolating inside for decades. The first person utters a soul-witnessing sad admittance which was unavoidable at their mutual level of hope, sadness, and despair, that provokes a dual gasp in the room, now a silent void.

The doctor walks into the room where you have been sitting, drowning in its deafening, hissing silence. You then hear the deliberate sentences stating things are "not as good as we had hoped." With head bowed your gasp is a prelude to an eternal silence, inevitable and witnessed by the one person who did everything they could to not be here.

A wedding: fervent vows with life's most intense gaze, delivered with such emotional joy and loving hesitation that your beautiful listener gasps in a blessed natural silence with eyes shining. The fifty people in attendance, witnessing, are simply wide-eyed, holding their breath.

A PERSONAL POMPEI

A good friend's young wife died in a sudden, tragic car accident sitting at an intersection.

A day like any other. Leaking sun that lifts us to coffee. A regular dwelling on what is still undone, what to address first, and what to hope for. Busy, behind, in a hurry, hoping not to forget something that will cause a furtive gasp or a U-turn to pick up a small presumed forgotten parcel of necessity. Sitting at a stop light, cogitating what is incomplete and complete, but always insufficient by my stellar standards of spit and polish.

I must see myself reflecting on its polished perfection at all times. I honk at the person in front of me who obviously does not have the requisite standards that demand immediate forward motion. It's inconceivable that I am still waiting, with rapid breath and shaking head, together with my duties. Then, an instantaneous huge shake, impact, and explosion that is somehow making my body evaporate instantly in real time.

I am now watching this unexpected eruption in stop action, slow mo, from within and above at the same time. I don't even have time to consider how or why I am inexorably going someplace ethereal and not to the daily work that I desire and passionately prescribe toy. I am not headed to the home that is my beautiful cave of light color filled with the people who make me regularly smile on the inside and out. A sudden flash, and I am not where I was or where I aimed to be just a few minutes from now, let alone the decades to come that I was counting on.

Noon, August 24, 79AD… Bright sun raining down on me in the market, taking care of business. I notice a familiar groan from Vesuvius, your old grumpy mound, you. But now you are yelling quite loudly, spittle rising high in the air, showing, this is more than your normal petulance. The old man is spitting wicked sputum that is just plain rude. We below shake off the resulting ash, pumice and volatile insults but then find the molten rock suddenly screaming at our doors. We started trying to run away, but after 20 hours, you vomited 20 feet of ash-icing on us, which made leaving very difficult. It is late night now and the lava is so fast moving and so hot that you fry us in our desperate stumbling steps and sleep. The city was gone,15,000 left visibly dead out of the 20,0000 that abided peacefully there. Starting as a normal day that got no regular apex but rather a one-of-a-kind incredibly tragic nadir.

March 9, 2022, where I am but one beautiful, anxious person at a random stoplight trying to get through pressed time to my job and passionate calling. Just like most of the ragged, cheerful, and sad people around me at this anonymous intersection. But in 2022, this personal Vesuvius is a quick personal aortic aneurysm within someone's innocent chest that does not mean to hurt me but who is dead at the wheel going 60mph.

The ancient Italian hours are now small Missouri seconds, happening behind me, unknowingly about to interrupt my agenda and alter my fate. There was a brief cluster of chaotic seconds and gasps from an unsuspecting poor soul who was now about to surprisingly jump to his next place. He did not even know what an aortic aneurism could feel like. Anyone who does never reports back.

The heavy body slumped onto the wheel with a dead foot slammed into the accelerator. This time, the tragedy is a flash of time and fire, not the warm days of spectacular plum of ash and pumice as it was back in 79AD.

An inconceivable, unexpected confluence of a quick, sad caprice that ended up smashing my innocent old car with me in it. To my sad surprise, leaving me now with a very sudden firm, glowing mission and responsibility to, inconceivably, reach back after this black flash to my loved people, whom I now suddenly realized even more, loved me even more than I loved them…which I did not think possible…. but here it is.

In this open, brutal flash of light, my life and heart experience a sudden relocation from normal to eternal, sitting at an intersection.

She took our breath away on a daily basis. She was demanding but was only asking us to be as good as she was always trying to be. Often only requesting a quicker pace than we might normally want but one that she regularly demanded of herself. Her energy was always making us huff, gasp, and laugh, and we always wanted to stay up with her and that smile. Her example of existence will never leave anyone who knew her. By her leaving that black bright day, she branded us all with that smile and joie de vivre.

TEXAS HISTORY

When I was in high school in Houston, I was required to take Texas History. Yea, like, is there a class taught in Illinois called "Illinois History"? Ok, I'm in High School so all I have to do is just show up to the class I was assigned. Now, I have to explain here: this class was after lunch, so we are talking about my Siesta time. Aside from that, while I loved history as a kid, Texas history was not enthralling to me. So, between the lack of curiosity and my predictable mid-day propensity for sacred naps, paying attention to this class was not on my agenda.

But, for some unknown reason, I always sat my soon somnambulant self in the front row of desks, right in the middle of the firing line of the riveting discourse that was Texas History. This unique teacher, whose name I do not recall, happened to put a clear, unexpected, photographic impression on my young mind at this time.

As I regularly nodded off in sweet, gentle slumber, I was serendipitously close enough to see his babbling, sincere, aged face in detail. I had never noticed the ability to look at old people, up to then, in any other way but hunger and fear. But this was an involuntarily microscopic inspection of wrinkles that I had not noticed before. Being so close, I became intrigued with the random old gray hairs that were scattered on his visage, unshaved." How could you miss that?!" said the smooth nubile coasting off to sleep a few feet away.

He always wore a suit that was worn but obviously loved and consecrated. Then there was the prerequisite tie, mounted on the thin frame of an old crisp shirt that could not really get crisp anymore. So, this is what proper teachers wore to represent taking teaching seriously, I thought. I respected this. He spoke with gentility and deep knowledge of his subject, but I always had an impression that he would have been rattling off dates and episodes fervently even if we were not there. He had such love for what he was doing that I don't think it really mattered who, or if, anyone was actually listening anymore. I found it perplexing but endearing.

I sensed his life joy was laying out ideas for youth. His tone of voice was always very sincere yet perfunctory, with a pungent smell of age and habit. But he still seemed to constantly revel in the art of teaching after those many years. He was going through extolling the Texas past without caring if the 40 ears in the room were really listening or caring.

I am sure he was hoping his wide-eyed enthusiasm would rub off on us or at least keep us awake. I don't think I was alone in dialing out with my relaxing naps, but because I was in front and asleep, I never really looked back to see who else might actually be enthralled or just drawing doodles or snoring along with me. As a new growth back then, I was just perplexed. But now, as an old growth, I see he was maintaining. Maintaining his passion, his profession, his days, and his purpose. What strikes me to this day is that he always did it with a glowing, positive expression and warm, gentle smile that was never directed to any person in particular but just to the ceiling universe that he usually looked up to. It was really the only one paying any attention, I think.

He was punched out with sincerity and the repetition of years but still in love and happily repeating his precious dogma, more often for himself than any real listener now. I think he knew in the past, he had ignited some Lone Star history fires, but today, he was not so sure. But still, every day, he always stepped up to the plate and swung with vigor and a smile. What I learned from this inconsequential midafternoon class/nap on Texas history was something his aged teaching did not intend. That once I woke up, I would have to start caring.

BUS OF FATE

There just seems to be too many times when disease and catastrophe show no respect at all for good intentions, diet, and sobriety. Lying there in the gutter, with my last ironic smile, after accidentally stepping in front of a bus while congratulating myself on the kale salad I recently digested and now left thinking that I should have just eaten the Oreo.

Mother Nature seems to just roll the dice sometimes, even if we are not in the game. Accidents happen. Hopefully, we can walk away and learn. All our best diets, exercise regimes, positive thoughts, and patience can usually keep us on a planned road of best intentions and some success, but we must not rule out the bus of fate. All we can do is look both ways carefully and step out. Relish now, taste now, embrace now. Take now with a smile. The dice are rolling even if we are not at the table.

TIME IS RUNNING OUT

What do you do when you sense your time is running out? Youth never contemplate oblivion.

Now, in this very experienced body, I unwillingly involuntarily, feast on memories. This has

allowed me to gain a heavily appreciated mottled skin and a precious soul weight of 7 plus decades. All the well cured pounds of bliss, wonderment, satisfaction, and regret allow me to observe a looming end to the road with relative peace.

But, no, not done yet. Bruised does not mean bled out. Just because the punches have blanketed the decades with some solid, deep purple impacts, that does not mean you have to lay down and look at the sky and say "bye."

Reinvent and capitalize on the hard-won library of yourself. Now you can finally stop and listen to all those screaming soft whispers that you ignored year after year. Appreciate and revel.

There is an open armed stare at the morning sun, in accepting age. We are not done; we are only unraveling.

WANT

There was a time when I did not know what was there, but there was want. There was a time later when I found something to aim for and found my weapon of desperation and desire. Then there was an epoch of "I can" and I do. One gets hooked on life as we set it up.

The habit of living as planned often has little peripheral vision so we miss bits of "can't" sneaking into the room. Then, the days of "can't" arrive bearing their own banal banners that we often feel well before we see their unfamiliar countenance and smell their tart, ripe airs. Then we can't. But all along, want stayed unparalleled and stalwart to all the days of strife and success. Want was there to pick me up, put sight in my eyes, a dream in my chest, and know when to rip the bandage off to get on with things. Want now makes an interesting companion to reminisce with.

When I Played the Horn

Chapter One

I am looking back, recently, on a decades-long career of horn that now, inexorably, selfishly, ignites my visceral desire to know its matrix. I often think what quick, ephemeral moment ignited my passion to play my soul song up a Fifth from the piano. A lot of time has passed now… uncountable concerts and untold ears have witnessed my efforts. But now, it has been so long without me holding the horn that you would have thought the amputated metal circles in F would have faded from my daily memory, steps, and breath. But that has not happened in spite of the dents and warm wells that it left in my soul.

Now, I want to try to explain and understand, for myself and any fellow lovers of our horn, the real plane that still looms in my aged library and maybe in your current daily pantry. Love does not stop. It just becomes alone and a warm memory on a shelf.

Click, I open the case to see this spherical mass of organized tubes exuding a radiance of a lifetime view, looking up a steep hill that I did not quite notice in all the starting intrigues, whispers, and passions. There is the intimacy of picking it up, with the innate required balanced two hands…the wonderment of svelte metal circles, with its wide head of glory: the bell. Now bring the long, extruding lead pipe with its introductory, inviting inserted mouthpiece to your lips. A cold metal kiss with thoughts of sonic passion explodes.

The very first, completely unfamiliar touch, as a novice, initiates an intimate request of the odd mouthpiece, leaving you wondering and breathless, "Why am I here…what in the world am I doing?" Now, you galvanize your singing soul and try to say "hello" with the voice of a musical collaborator that you just met. You were intrigued, in the near past, with some resonant soul called the horn that you heard somewhere and asked yourself, "Can I sing like what I heard?"

You start on an open-ended quest to tame the unnatural execution and dream of exuding beauty in spite of all its pratfalls. The new adopted family of lip muscles talking to the dream sound in our head in the language of an air/muscle discussion is not a predictable road you quickly find out. We individual players/lovers, all have tempered dreams and an unlimited variation of challenges to sing the metal. Teeth, jaw, posture, and natural resistance to some foreign musical machine that is now pressing on my face by beloved choice.

Each day, perseverance is the teacher. Each day, the stubborn dream of those bounteous harmonics lures us to the music stand in some solitary room. Overcoming unseen inadequacies and weakness takes pools of imagination and courage to keep taking it out of the case day by day, breathing the airs of dread and hope. We do it for the dream. We do it because, within our personal insatiable sonic lust, we are enticed to go on with a Siren Song, fueled only with bare random patches of improvement and beauty that our stubbornness has let us experience. As we actually briefly revel and improve within this sadomasochistic adopted family, we make unique, inspiring moments that, thankfully, touch our own souls and, magically, others in the nearby.

Chapter Two

Decades of breathing the horn, in all its vicissitudes and joys, led me to think I had complete knowledge and control just because I let my hot passion spill daily in front of a music stand. I actually could do anything the horn asked me to do for a beautiful, generous time that left me breathless and humble every day. Little did I know that deep pool of expertise welded an insufficient armor against some of Mother Nature's mysterious weapons. Beneath the bounteous garden I had cultivated of colorful growth, strength, and fecund control, I learned that things could slowly shift sideways at the same time. Infrequently, small momentary weeds started to appear in my playing, not causing anything other than query and a silent head turn, "odd." Then, things started to catapult into unrecognizable episodes and spasms that had nothing to do with the catechism of knowledge that I knew and had unwaveringly supported me. Nothing related to the normal signs of not paying attention to the regular challenges of playing the horn. Strange sensations of my lip existence appeared that I had never felt in my daily decades of meditating and hugging my beloved horn. I tried all the answers in my experienced gut and then started to follow some medical and pedagogical suggestions.

I came to find out that Dystonia is a hydrahead of subtlety and shock. This led to a gradually narrow, dark dirt road that had me standing there, being less of a player than I was when I started 50 years ago. I thought I knew everything about playing the horn. I dug deep for decades and pulled the gems that worked for me and many others but could not have planned for Mother Nature's slap of Enlightenment called Dystonia. No rules, no logic based on what I knew as the horn, your stalwart mysterious adversary now playing in a boxing ring with no gloves.

The innocent hubris I had bred within myself by simply cajoling and wrestling with the horn for decades did not, even remotely, help me deal with the Armageddon of the nerves in my face suddenly not correctly hearing my screaming brain. Embouchure now short circuiting, in a Whack a Mole fashion, that had no points of reference to the natural cause and effect I had demanded and learned over my long career.

After exhausting all the pedagogical and medical perspectives, I was left standing in my home studio one October morning, saying to my beloved horn, "I am sorry, buddy, we are done. It was a great ride. Thank you, but we're finished." The bandage horn that had been my costume and shield in life was gone. It was not a normal attrition of age, fatigue, boredom, or any normal frailty.

It was a nightmare that I could not wake up from with the horn in my hands. The only way to wake up was to put it in the case and never open it again. As painful as it was, the horn and I at least parted on compassionate, friendly terms, knowing that it was neither of our faults. It was out of our hands. Now I look back and thank the Fates who allowed me to play the horn, making it a significant part of my soul whether I am making sound or not.

JAY KENT HACKLEMAN

I saved this prose for the end because it best demonstrates my creative process.

I wrote this on the plane going home from my father's funeral.
After, you will see the scribbled notes, and then the formatting done by my. brother, Scott.

"I know the dirty fingernails of demons and gods you have only dreamt of."

The moment he opened the casket, I knew you were not there. You were gleaming from the picture frames on display on either side of the box. The sleeping slack mouth was neither pensive, loquacious, or smiling; it could not have been you. Your real face was hovering as a faint reflection in that mesmerizing black and white picture of open sea waves that hangs in your living room. That was your fathers.

You stared at it like your dad, I'm sure; it was one of his favorites, too. Your presence is palpable in the east- west glances of your beloved dog Rufus. Some clothes hang in your closet with a little dirt and the expectancy of maybe tomorrow's inevitable sigh of a later wash. That yard at Hazleton was a constant struggle, but when you witnessed its timbres with poking and raking, you applauded its Nature songs. You loved being not inside.

Your study reeks of your conscience. Early on, I sensed your impatience. At first, I thought it was with me, but of course it wasn't. You were mostly impatient with yourself for not being strong enough to shift the world around you. Maybe deep down in a naked little corner, you were a bit irritated that, at the very least, you were not stalwart enough not to care.

You instinctively wanted to share your priorities. You gave us a fierce respect of expression. Music speaks for me most often, and you saw my passion as illogical but felt its inevitable begrudgingly. Your pride in my success warmed you greatly. Scott tried to emulate you almost unconsciously and was often loved severely.

Georgia was so nearby. You two were like two large stones rubbing against one another, seemingly inseparable.

Amy just had to make you happy. Laurie loves you dearly and never really understood why. Doris can appreciate the panorama of your growth, a unique pleasure even after the bitter divorce. We all envied and pitied Sharon because she had the best and worst of all worlds. She was shaken and caressed.

I was bad in keeping in touch, but you are still like an underground stream in my soul. You liked to hear the babble, but I rarely felt the need because I always felt the moisture.

That shop is an eternal honing of your existence. Nothing within your reach stayed the same save nature, which you took pains to try and float across, witness, and protect.

I don't know all the moments of bodily functions and obvious mistakes. As a son those are behind the valance of parenthood. I borrowed two pair of your shoes today, but I will never fill them. No one is perfect, but one gets the closest when they leave. You were very close to us all, even if we were not together too often, and you could be very exasperating to be around.

I am sorry you left so soon, but for what it's worth, you could have left a long time ago and still have been immortal.

— Jay Kent Hackleman —

... I know the dirty fingernails of demons and gods you have only dreamt of ...

The moment he opened the casket, I knew you were not there.
You were gleaming from the frames on display on either side of the box.
The sleeping slack mouth was neither Pensive, Loquacious, nor Smiling; it could not have been you.
Your real face was hovering as a faint reflection in that mezmerising black and white picture of open sea waves
that hangs in your living room. You stared at it like your Dad would have.
Your presence is palpable in the east-west glances of Rufus. Some clothes hang in your closet with a little dirt
and the expectancy of tomorrow's bends
and the inevitable sigh of a later wash.

That yard at Hazelton is a constant struggle, but at least when you witnessed its timbers with poking and raking
you applauded its songs as best could be done.

Your study reeks of your conscience.
Early on I sensed your impatience. At first I thought it was with me, but of course it wasn't.
You were mostly impatient with yourself for not being able to shift the world around you. Maybe deep down
in a naked little corner you were a bit irritated that at the very least you were not stalwart enough not to care.

You instinctively wanted to share your priorities. You gave us a fierce respect of expression.
Music speaks for me most often, and a taciturn example follows in the tacets.
Scott tried to emulate almost unconsciously and was loved severely always.
Georgia was so near; like two stones rubbing against one another and seemingly inseparable.
Amy just had to make you happy.
Lori loves you dearly and never really understood why.
Neal's timing left him with a distance he spanned with more than respect.
Doris can appreciate the panorama of your growth; a unique pleasure.
We all envied and pitied Sharon because she had the best and worst of all worlds.

I was bad at keeping in touch. You are like an underground stream in my soul.
You liked to hear the babble, but I rarely felt the need because I always felt the moisture.

That shop; an eternal honing of your existence. Nothing within your reach stayed the same,
save nature, which you took pains to try and float across, witness, and protect.

I don't know all the bodily functions and obvious mistakes.
In your case there was so much more that overshadowed the inevitable.
I borrowed two pairs of your shoes today. I will never fill them.
No one is perfect, but one gets closest when they leave.
You were very close, very exasperating, when you were around.
I am sorry you left so soon, but for what it's worth you could have left a long time ago
and still have been immortal.

Marty Hackleman 2.5.98
10pm AirCanada flt.9013 Houston-Vancouver

~~I HAVE KNOWN THE~~
DIRTY FINGERNAILS OF DEMONS AND GODS
YOU HAVE ONLY DREAMT OF ~~Rage~~

2/1/98

THE MOMENT HE OPENED THE CASKET I KNEW YOU WERE NOT THERE. YOU WERE GLEAMING FROM THE FRAMED MOMENTS ON DISPLAY ON EITHER SIDE OF THE BOX. THE SLEEPING SLACK MOUTH WAS NEITHER PENSIVE, LOQUASCIOUS, OR SMILING; IT COULD NOT HAVE BEEN YOU. YOUR REAL FACE WAS HOVERING AS A REFLECTION IN THAT MEZMERIZING BLACK AND WHITE PICTURE OF OPEN-SEA WAVES. YOU STARED AT IT LIKE YOUR DAD I'M SURE. YOUR PRESENCE IS PALPABLE IN THE EAST-WEST GLANCES OF RUFUS. SOME CLOTHES HANG IN YOUR CLOSET WITH A LITTLE DIRT AND THE EXPECTANCY OF TOMORROW'S BENDS AND AN SIGH OF A INEVITABLE LATER WASH.

THAT YARD AT HAZELTON IS A CONSTANT STRUGGLE BUT AT LEAST WHEN YOU WITNESSED ITS TAMBERS WITH POKING AND RACKING YOU ~~TOTALY RELISHED~~ APPLAUDED ITS SONGS AS BEST COULD BE DONE.

YOUR STUDY REEKS OF YOUR CONSCIENCE. EARLY ON I SENSED YOUR IMPATIENCE. AT FIRST I OF COURSE THOUGHT IT WAS WITH ME BUT IT WASN'T. YOU WERE MOSTLY IMPATIENT WITH YOURSELF FOR NOT BEING STRONG ENOUGH TO SHIFT THE WORLD AROUND YOU. MAYBE DEEP DOWN IN A CORNER A BIT IRRITATED THAT AT THE VERY LEAST YOU WERE NOT STALWART ENOUGH NOT TO CARE.

YOU INSTINCTIVLY WANTED TO SHARE YOUR PRIORITIES. YOU GAVE US ~~Rage~~ A FIERCE

RESPECT OF EXPRESSION. I DO IT MOSTLY WITH MY MUSIC AND TRY WITH MY EXAMPLE. SCOTT TRIED TO EMULATE ALMOST UNCONSCIOUSLY AND WAS LOVED SEVERELY ALWAYS. GEORGIA WAS SO NEAR; LIKE TWO LARGE STONES, FRICTIONS WITH THE PRESSURE. AMY HAD TO MAKE YOU HAPPY, LAURIE LOVES YOU BARELY AND NEVER REALLY UNDERSTOOD WHY. DORIS CAN APPRECIATE THE PANORAMA OF YOUR GROWTH AND HAD A UNIQUE PLEASURE, WE ALL ENVIED AND PITIED SHARON BECAUSE SHE HAD THE BEST AND WORST OF ALL WORLDS;

I WAS BAD IN KEEPING IN TOUCH. YOU ARE LIKE AN UNDERGROUND STREAM IN MY SOUL; YOU LIKED TO HEAR THE BABBLE BUT I RARELY FELT THE NEED BECAUSE I ALWAYS FELT THE MOISTURE.

THAT SHOP; AN ETERNAL HONING OF YOUR EXISTANCE, NOTHING WITHIN YOUR REACH STAYED THE SAME DAVE NATURE WOULD YOU TOOK PAINS TO TRY AND FLOAT ACCROSS, WITNESS, AND PROTECT.

I DON'T KNOW ALL THE MOMENTS OF BODILY FUNCTIONS AND OBVIOUS MISTAKES. IN YOUR CASE THERE WAS SO MUCH MORE THAT OVERSHADOWED THE INEVITABLE,

Continental (3)

In Flight With

I BORROWED TWO PAIR OF YOUR SHOES TODAY. I WILL NEVER FILL THEM. NO ONE IS PERFECT BUT ONE GETS CLOSEST WHEN THEY LEAVE. YOU WERE VERY CLOSE, VERY EXASPERATING WHEN YOU WERE AROUND. I AM SORRY YOU LEFT SO SOON BUT FOR WHAT IT'S WORTH YOU COULD HAVE LEFT A LONG TIME AGO AND STILL HAVE BEEN IMMORTAL.

MARTY HACKLMAN
2/5/98

REFLECTIONS

RESONANCE

GROWING UP: REMEMBER SMELL, HANDS
SENSE OF WISDOM + EXPERIENCE
"... I KNOW THE DIRTY FINGERNAILS OF
DEMONS AND GODS YOU HAVE ONLY
DREAMT OF."

~~OOOO~~ OFTEN SEEMED IMPATIENT: MOSTLY W/HIMSELF
FOR NOT BEING STRONG ENOUGH TO SHIFT
THE WORLD AROUND HIM OR STALWART
ENOUGH TO NOT CARE.
BUT HE ALWAYS CARED.
~~OFTEN SEEMED~~ A BIT TORTURED ~~MANY~~ AT TIMES
BUT WAS ALWAYS DEARLY SEEKING PEACE
OFTEN FOUND IT IN SOME PEOPLES EYE
MOST DOGS, AND ALL OF NATURE.

LOVED LATIN ...
TUUM EST - IT'S UP TO YOU

(A) That did not make them perfect but christ, were they convincing.

(B) That stop. ~~An~~ eternal homing of your existance. ~~N~~othing within your reach stayed the same ~~save the~~ nature which ~~~~ you took pains to ~~~~ ~~try and~~ float accross, ~~~~ ~~~~ witness and ~~~~ protest.

(D) ~~GOES HERE~~ ~~I dont to~~ know all the moments of bodily functions and obvious mistakes. In your case there was so much more ~~that~~ overshadowing the ~~~~ inevitable (E) ~~~~ ~~N~~o one is perfect but one gets closest ~~~~ when they leave. But you were very close, very ~~exasperating~~ when you were around. I am sorry you left so soon ~~~~ but for what its worth you could have left a long time ago and still have been immortal.

(C) We all ~~envied~~ and pitied ~~Sharon~~; she had the best and worst of all worlds. (D) GOES HERE

_____

The moment he opened the casket I knew you were not there. You were gleaming from the framed moments ~~one~~ on display an center seat of its box, ~~for~~ the slack mouth was neither sleeping pensive, ~~but~~ ~~say~~ loquacious, or smiling; it ~~a~~ couldn't have been you. Your real face was ~~too~~ back in the living room ~~faintly~~ ~~known~~ hovering as a reflection in that mesmerizing black and white picture of open sea women. You stared at it like your ~~&~~ Dad I'm sure, although ~~you'd~~ ~~were~~ ~~seen~~ J.C. stare at . Your presence is palpable in the ~~east-west~~ glance of Rufus.

(B) ~~I~~ borrowed the pair of your shoes the day I figured out. ~~are~~ I will never fill them.

(V) That yard at Hazelton is a constant struggle but at least when you witnessed its timbres, poking and raking, ~~you~~ ~~has~~ ~~sea~~ relished it songs, (V) ~~You~~ stuff reeks of your conscience. as best could be done.

Early on I sensed your impatience. At first I of course thought it was with me but it was not really. You were mostly impatient with yourself for not being strong enough to ~~sto~~ ~~change~~ the world around you or far deep down maybe irritated that you were not stalwart enough to just ~~not~~ care. ~~Your~~ ~~priorities~~ ~~You instinctively want~~ to share your priorities. (A) ~~you~~ ~~wanted~~ ~~to~~ share. You gave us kids a fierce respect of expression. I do it mostly with my music and try with my example. Scott tried to emulate her closely and was ~~very~~ ~~always~~ lonesome severely, always. Georgia was so close; friction prior almost unconsciously near

(D)

I was bad for keeping in touch. You are
like an underground stream in my soul;
you listen to hear the babble but
~~a brother~~ I rarely felt the need because
I always felt the moisture, TO (E)

At 72 a split aorta filled my father's
~~breast~~ breast with blood in his sleep and took
him from us quickly even though he was
in good health. I wrote these things
coming home on the plane.

AT 72 A SPLIT AORTA FILLED MY FATHERS
BREAST WITH BLOOD IN HIS SLEEP AND
STOLE HIM FROM US IN SPITE OF HIS
(OBVIOUS) GOOD HEALTH, I WROTE THESE
~~THOUGHTS~~ COMMING HOME ON THE PLANE
IN THE ~~OR~~ DARKNESS AND NOISE OF A
NIGHT FLIGHT + LONELINESS, MAYBE SOME
WORDS MAY STRIKE A RESONANCE
WITH SOME OF YOUR READERS THAT

ADDENDUM

In addition to the poem about my father, I thought it would be interesting to the reader to offer samples of other works in progress. You will notice a sampling of writing on the back of parking tickets. When there was down time, I would often jot down ideas for my poems on the only thing I had at hand, which were the parking tickets from the fancy eatery where I worked as a teenager. I had my little black bow tie and thin jacket that I would wear while running around parking and retrieving cars for patrons. I usually worked from five to midnight or so, and only for tips. It was Houston, so I really learned to sweat.

I still have all my typed poems in this Rag-tag, messy birthing style. I am also finding there are a number of works I never typed for some reason or another. When I started writing, it was out of the blue and quickly became an obsession. It helped get me through those universal tumultuous years we all experience when we're young. I was my worst and best confidant, friend, and teacher, but we all, somehow, made it to the different joys and pratfalls of adulthood, a little surprised and bruised.

I am still learning.

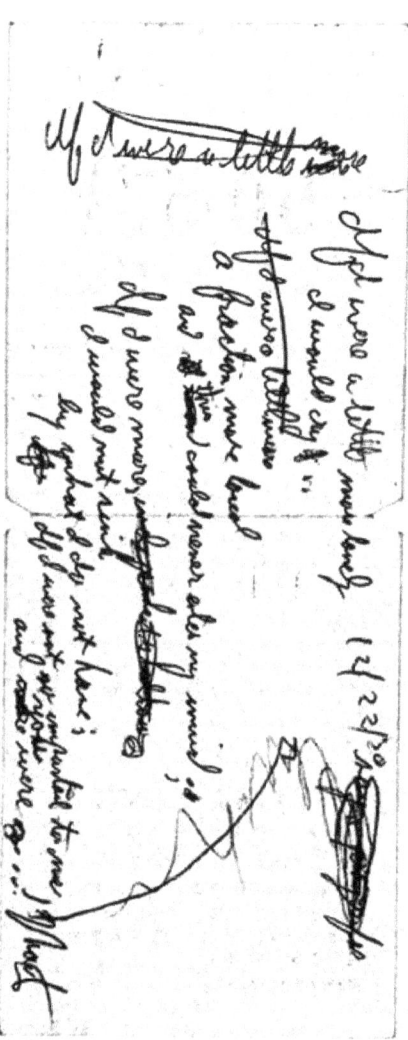

6/22/70

With a whiffsy laugh
~~that~~ they pass
into the night,
into the night,
~~the~~ the tree top veil
~~that covers;~~
Who a sound!
an echo faithless to
and destined to die...

If I were a little more

If I were a little more
I would ask ..
If I were taller
a faster, more hel
If I were many
I would not mind
... could never alter my mind;
by what I do not have;
If I was not ...
and ... were g ...

10/22/70

Hark
the night a reprieve
from the ... arms
of a combatant day;
the jelly called daylight
sometimes kills ..

None are not spared
their shackled emotions
in branded, branded
days
no solstice bread
for theirs is no limit;

perhaps more lonely
than the lonely
are the loved;
for theirs is an addicted ...
whilst mine ...
of cherishing what'd have too ...

1/29/70

1/27/70

i saw a dog
 laid prostrate
 by death along the road this morn..
 ~~only~~ ~~it~~ ~~is baking~~
 the sun ~~its motionless~~ ~~fore~~ eternity
  ~~binds~~ ~~along the~~ pavement..
out the suns flies ~~and it~~ setting upon
 its inflamed instantaneous horror
 there cast upon the metalic path..;
and streaming like steel tears around the corpse,
 the breathing iron ~~flew~~ run close to a marathon.
 ~~it~~ in speedy memoriam;.
  the pistons humming an elegy
   by the thousands..

www.ingramcontent.com/pod-product-compliance
Lightning Source LLC
Chambersburg PA
CBHW051628140626
46547CB00033B/2834